Giraffes

Contents

Introducing Giraffes	2
What Do Giraffes Look Like?	4
Giraffe Species	10
How Giraffes Move and Communicate	14
How and Where Giraffes Live	18
Glossary	24

Written by Tracey Reeder

Introducing Giraffes

Giraffes are the tallest of all living animals. Their name comes from a word that means *one who walks fast.*

Giraffe Names

Long ago people thought giraffes were a cross between leopards and camels. They called them camelopards.

Xiapha is an old Arabic word. It means *one who walks fast.*

The scientific name for giraffes is *Giraffa camelopardalis.*

What Do Giraffes Look Like?

horn

ear

neck

mane

vertebrae

nostril

tongue

fur

knee pad

hoof

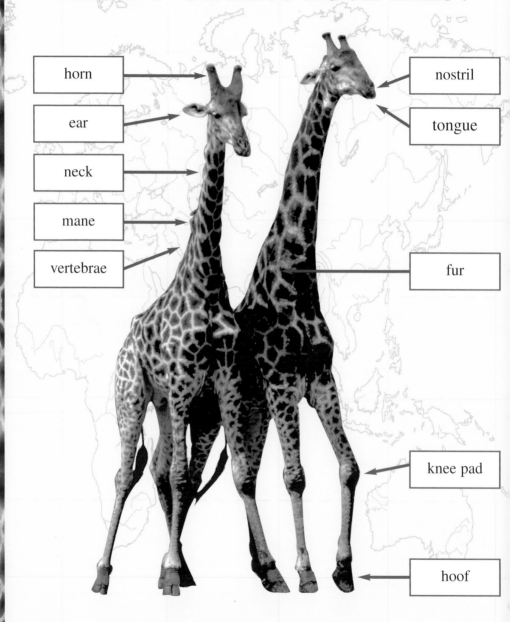

Male giraffes are called bulls. Bull giraffes can grow to about 16 to 20 feet (490 cm – 600 cm) tall. Male giraffes' legs can be between 8 to 10 feet (245 cm – 300 cm) long, and their necks about 6 to 7 feet (180 cm – 215 cm) long.

Female giraffes are called cows. Cows are usually about 2 to 3 feet (60 cm – 90 cm) shorter than male giraffes.

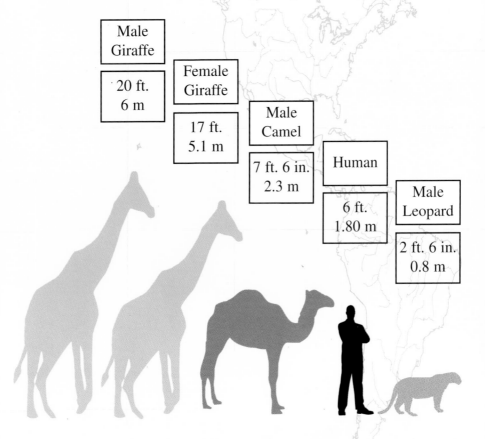

Male Giraffe

20 ft.
6 m

Female Giraffe

17 ft.
5.1 m

Male Camel

7 ft. 6 in.
2.3 m

Human

6 ft.
1.80 m

Male Leopard

2 ft. 6 in.
0.8 m

Giraffe Necks

Giraffe necks are very long but they do not have lots of bones in them. The bones that are in a giraffe's neck are at least 10 inches (25 cm) long. It is these long bones that make a giraffe's neck very stiff.

Giraffes have manes on their necks. The hairs in the giraffe's mane are short and stiff.

Giraffe Bodies and Feet

Giraffe bodies are covered with fur. The skin on a giraffe's knees is very hard. The skin is hard so that the giraffe does not hurt its knees when it is resting on stony ground.

Sitting down is hard for a giraffe.

Giraffes have hooves. Each hoof is split into two toes. Giraffe hooves are very strong so that giraffes can run over hard rocks and ground.

Giraffe Horns

Giraffes have horns. The male giraffe has bigger horns than the female giraffe. The horns grow out of the top of the giraffe's head. The horns are covered with skin and hair.

Giraffe Tongues

Giraffes have long tongues. The tongues can grow up to 20 inches (50 cm) long. Giraffes use their tongues and upper lips to pull leaves from trees.

Giraffe Senses

Giraffes have very good eyesight. Their good eyesight and long necks help giraffes see their enemies. Giraffes have very good hearing. This helps them hear their enemies in time to run away. Giraffes also have special nostrils. They can close their nostrils to keep out dust and sand.

Attributes of a Giraffe

Good eyesight → Seeing enemies

Long necks → Getting food from tall trees

Long necks → Seeing enemies

Long tongues → Pulling leaves to eat

Special nostrils → Close to keep out dust

Knee pads → For resting on stony ground

Tough hooves → For running on hard rocks

Tough hooves → For fighting enemies

Long vertebrae → To make their necks stiff

Giraffe Species

Masai giraffe

Reticulated giraffe

Rothschild giraffes

There is only one species of giraffe, but there are many sub-species. Each subspecies lives in a different part of Africa. Most of the time you can tell a subspecies of giraffe by the pattern and shade of the giraffe's fur and spots. Sometimes it is hard to tell which subspecies a giraffe belongs to because giraffe groups mix and have babies.

A mother giraffe licking her baby.

Giraffe Subspecies

Name of Giraffe	Shade of Spots
Masai	Dark chocolate
Baringo/Rothschild	Deep brown
Nubian	Chestnut brown
Cape	Dark brown
Kordofan	Chestnut brown
Reticulated	Red-brown

Some Other Giraffes
- Nigerian giraffes live in Chad.
- Angolan giraffes live in Angola and Zambia.
- Thornicroft giraffes live in Zambia.

Shape of Spots	Shade of Coat	Where They Live
Jagged edge	Yellow	Kenya Tanzania
Blotchy rectangles	Cream	Uganda Kenya
Large four-sided	Off-white	Sudan Congo
Rounded blotch	Tan	South Africa, Zimbabwe, Namibia, Mozambique
Uneven smaller blotch	Off-white	Sudan
Large square	White	Kenya, Ethiopia, Somalia

Did You Know?
- Did you know that no two giraffes have the same pattern of spots?
- A giraffe's spots help make it hard for enemies to see the giraffe.

How Giraffes Move and Communicate

Giraffes can gallop at 35 mph (56 kmph).

Giraffes walk by moving both legs on one side of their body forward and then both the legs on the other side of their body. When giraffes run fast or gallop they swing both back legs forward at the same time. The back legs land outside the front legs. Giraffes can move as fast as 35 miles (56 km) per hour.

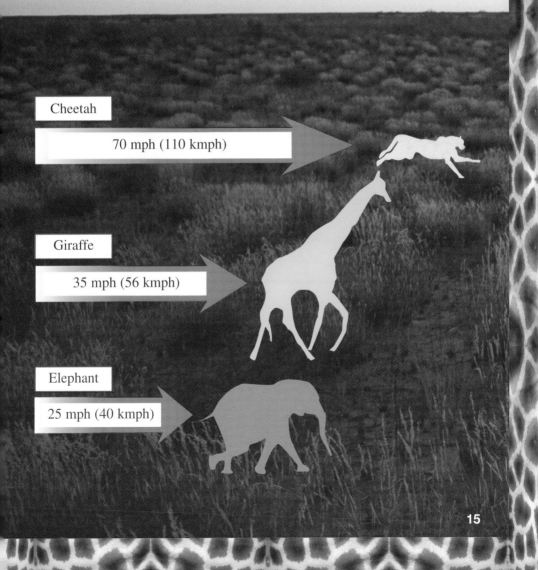

Cheetah
70 mph (110 kmph)

Giraffe
35 mph (56 kmph)

Elephant
25 mph (40 kmph)

Giraffes have to lower their necks to drink.

Because giraffes' legs and necks are so long, they have to be very careful not to break them. Getting up and sitting down is not easy for giraffes so they usually sleep standing up. When giraffes do sit down, they often rest their long necks on a low tree branch.

When they want to drink, giraffes have to spread their front legs very far apart so they can get their mouth down far enough to reach the water.

Giraffe Sounds

Giraffes make very low grunting sounds. These sounds are so low it is hard for people to hear the sound. For a long time people thought giraffes made no sound at all.

Giraffes make low grunting sounds.

How and Where Giraffes Live

Africa

Where Giraffes Live

Giraffes live in the open woodlands and wooded grass areas of Africa. Today most giraffes live in game parks. Game parks are places where people are not allowed to hunt animals.

Key (Legend)

Angola		Somalia	
Chad		South Africa	
Congo		Sudan	
Ethiopia		Tanzania	
Kenya		Uganda	
Namibia		Zambia	
Mozambique		Zimbabwe	

Giraffe Life Cycles

Giraffes are mammals. A mammal is a warm-blooded animal that gives birth to its young and feeds them milk. Female giraffes carry their babies inside them for 15 months. The mother giraffe gives birth to its baby standing up. The baby giraffe has to drop up to 6 feet (1.8 m) to reach the ground.

Baby giraffes are called calves. When calves are born, they weigh around 150 pounds (68 kg) and stand 6 feet tall (1.8 m). Calves have to learn to stand up and walk as soon as they are born. They drink their mother's milk and start to eat leaves in the first months of their life. Most giraffes live for about 25 years.

Mother giraffes feed their babies milk.

What Giraffes Eat

Giraffes eat leaves. They also eat flowers, vines and herbs. They do not eat meat. Giraffes spend 16 – 20 hours each day eating but they can go for weeks without drinking water.

Ruminants
Giraffes are ruminants. A ruminant is an animal that brings food back up from its stomach and chews it again. This is called chewing cud.

Giraffe Families

Giraffes live with other giraffes in small herds. Most of the herd is made up of female giraffes and their calves. Herds tend to stay in the same place. This place can be as large as 46 square miles (120 square kilometers).

Male giraffes often fight with other male giraffes to show how strong they are. Giraffes use their long legs to protect themselves. When an enemy attacks a giraffe, the giraffe will kick out with its legs and feet or run away as fast as it can. Some giraffe enemies are lions, hyenas, leopards, and wild dogs.

Glossary

Cud is the name for a ball of chewed food animals called ruminants bring back into their mouths to chew again.

When animals with four legs run fast, they **gallop**.

Giraffa camelopardalis is the scientific name for giraffes.

A **herd** is a name for a group of animals who live together.

Mammals are animals which give birth to live babies who feed on their mother's milk.

The openings in an animal's face which are used for breathing in air are called **nostrils**.

Ruminants are animals with special stomachs who chew cud.

A **species** is a group of living things who all share the same characteristics. A **subspecies** is a subset of a species.

Land covered with grass and trees is called a **woodland**.